Velvet Eclipse

Velvet Eclipse

Samira Vivette

Velvet Eclipse
Copyright © 2024 Samira Vivette

All rights reserved.

No part of this book may be used or reproduced in any manner whatsoever without written permission from the Author, except in the case of reprints in the context of reviews.

ISBN: 978-0-6451638-8-9

A poetry and prose collection for souls on the twin flame journey, delving into thoughts, sentiments, and possibilities with passionate longing and intensity.

I wish for these words to capture the certainty, the doubt, the nights spent overthinking with unbearable yearning, and moments entertaining throwing the towel in against all feeling and logic. Some pieces will be confronting, others conflicting, enveloping passion, and patience, and faith in connection. Above all, I hope you feel comforted in knowing what is yours will never wander forever, and you know in the depths of your soul if they are the one for you.

With three chapters exploring each stage of twin flame separation, a stronger focus surrounds the second phase, with emphasis on the emotions which consume one's being in the moments of emotional ascension, experiencing a spiritual awakening, knowing in the depths of your being, and… waiting.

Allow these words to guide you on a journey within your soul, holding you close, keeping you warm with the assurance that you will always be reunited with what is yours.

Phases

The Collision...   *2*

The Separation...   *25*

The Reunion...   *105*

The Collision…

Nothing could have prepared me for it.

You think you've seen it all, having experienced the highs and lows of attachment, opening your heart to another, being someone who has loved and lost countless times before.

But it takes one connection to be thrown off course,
to make you question everything you've ever known.

During the time I met you, I underwent one of the biggest transformations of my life. I had always been a dreamer long before you came into the picture, and it was this aspect of my personality that would be my lifeline after your departure.

I was never expecting to meet myself in another body.
I could never anticipate being confronted by my wounds, triggers, and unhealed facets with such vigor that it led to myself breaking, healing, and thriving over and over again.

I had to nurture the parts of myself that weren't pleasant.
I had to comfort myself during the wreckage of your departures and recurrent reappearances. There were times I didn't think
I'd make it.

The magnetism that coursed through our veins was unlike anything I've ever felt. I am forever grateful for the lessons inflicted by your presence and absence. It is a blessing to have known you. And on a deeper level, now I truly know myself and what I am made of.

Samira Vivette

When I think of life before you, I think of all the beautiful people I've known and loved. I think of all the times I got it right, and all the times I messed up beyond belief. I think about every familiar face in a public crowd who reminded me of a friend in a past life, the kind of moments shared that ignite déjà vu and electrify one's skin with the possibility of infinity. I think about how fortunate I am to have lived such an enriching life, bursting with heartbreak and lessons to last a century – with tears, and letters, and gifts standing on my bedside table radiating melancholic memories. And when I think of life after you, my only thought is, *this entire time, where had you been?* How had I navigated this world in all its beauty, never having known you exist?

Velvet Eclipse

Darling, shall we capture the embers of infinity and create our own reality away from the vanishing spark of monotony? May we embody the limitless abyss and climb mountain peaks together with entwined fingertips, our irises reflecting our futures with uncertainty? As we trace our desires across the napes of our necks, let us melt and force ourselves to forget what comes next. Let us lose ourselves in what is not understood yet.

Samira Vivette

Let's give
each other
a part of
one another
to remember
for a slice
of forever.

Velvet Eclipse

Connecting with you is like connecting with myself on a level I never knew existed.

Forgive me for falling into us so passionately, so wholeheartedly.

I've never known anything like this.

Samira Vivette

I know you feel it too. I know the level of intensity between us has paved the way toward something you never thought existed. It's difficult for me to express what I feel without coming across as too much, but I am too much.

And I know you love that.

Velvet Eclipse

Brokenness has never concerned me.
The flawless façade has never intrigued me.

I don't look at you any differently for being human –
for experiencing hardships, messing up, and showcasing your vulnerability. To me, that is what living is about.
I appreciate your complexities, the grays, the in-between.
I will be here to listen to the thoughts which are too heavy to keep inside, to help you confront the demons you hide, to hold you especially close on the nights you require warmth and understanding, to ignite the kind of compassion that cradles the aches until they dissipate.

And our bones, they know.
They know we share something special.

Samira Vivette

And I know what I have with you is the closest I've ever been to grasping a pure connection because it feels nothing like all those other times that carved my insides and left me to bleed out on the carpet.

Velvet Eclipse

There are connections. And there are *connections*.

There are smiles and peaceful auras which scratch the surface, reflecting a gentle, steady glow – and there are divine entanglements that alter one's perception with kaleidoscopic intensity, clawing themselves within a soul permanently. When two people become enthralled in everything they never felt was missing, their essence is never the same again.

These connections are few and far between, and some in this lifetime are not granted the privilege of such a meeting.

This is an awakening that never leaves one the same again.

Samira Vivette

The passion we shared
from the moment we met
and every one thereafter
remained enveloped in magic
because I always knew…

It's always going to be you.

Velvet Eclipse

Consider my blessings counted
because the chances of our paths
crossing were a million to one.

We were the ones who defied all odds.

The Heart Nebula

It's dangerous to feel this much.
I am aware such intensity is usually fleeting.
But this time, it's different.
For you, I swear,
I would do anything.
Your presence induces
a cataclysmic infliction
where I lose all inhibition.
This magnetism is addictive.
Delightfully destructive.
And I know I'm a lot.
My passion consumes me in waves.
And I'm a lot to handle most days.
But never will I neglect us.
If only you could see yourself
through my eyes and feel this
familiarity beaming in my chest.
I promise, I don't see you
the way you see yourself.
My lips reassure your scars
in the same way your scars
reassure me that I have finally
met a soul who understands me,
equally.

And before
I fall asleep tonight,
you should probably know
that you're my final
and favorite thought.

Samira Vivette

I know we are special.

It's all in the non-verbal.

Velvet Eclipse

I see myself in you. And I know you do too because I cannot help but feel at home within your gaze as it pierces mine with a sense of perpetual patience, understanding, and oneness – you notice everything I have never acknowledged. Every hue of unexpressed desolation, every speck of reserved infatuation. This magnetism between us is not a manifestation of my imagination. I know you see through everything everybody never cared to fight for. I know you know that this, right here, is something inconceivably special.

Samira Vivette

I don't let many people in.
But you.
You were different.
Your energy meshed perfectly with mine.
It was an instant recognition.
A passionate connection.
Something other-worldly.
A spiritual familiarity.
Home in another body.

Velvet Eclipse

There isn't
a single thought
in my day
that is not entwined
with some aspect
of you.

Samira Vivette

And I won't ever stop thinking,
remembering, writing about you.

At least one of us
has to keep us alive.

Mystical.
Transcendental.
A shared exchange of uncertainties,
dreams, and acquainted suffering
by two energies reconciling in
another lifetime with the chance
to try again once more.

Samira Vivette

It's just another day.
It's just another night
where my thoughts
are tied to you and I.

Velvet Eclipse

If I could stop
thinking
about you,
I would.
If I could stop
writing
about you,
I would.
This is not
a typical,
overinflated,
surface-level
crush.
This was
an awakening
that completely
and entirely
messed
me up.

Samira Vivette

My Assurance

I'm not going anywhere.
I promise.
I know what it feels like for people to leave.
I know what it's like to hold onto belief that someone
out there will finally mean what they say and stay.

I've held onto hope longer than humanly possible
for it to slip between my fingers.
I've experienced suffering unimaginable.
I'm always the last one standing.
I'm the one who sees the potential,
not only what exists in front of me.
I'm someone who keeps my word.
I'm never going anywhere.
I'm here for you.

The Separation...

Velvet Eclipse

How delicate we ended up being.

We pulled ourselves across ruthless terrain,
uncovered our complexities together,
transcended everything surface-level,
acquainted ourselves within
our own little world where we
could make sense of our traumas,
be the villains together,
fuck our lives up together.

None of it had to make sense.
And it didn't.

You were my little slice of safety
because for once in my life,
someone finally understood me.

And it seems, just as easily,
you were taken from me.

Samira Vivette

It's almost midnight, and yet again, these late-night thoughts are here to do what they do best. I don't think my chest has known weightlessness since you left. My heart is a stranger to peace. I don't think there's any part of me that is tired of scraping the barrel of memories and preserving us, or at least what is left. But the remnants are fading. My gosh, they are fading. It's absolutely fucking terrifying, so here I am again… writing to keep the momentum flowing. It's not like anything can make it stop anyway. It's not like I want it to either.

Velvet Eclipse

And I'm using the days to try to let go of you.

But the nights don't want me to.

Samira Vivette

Did we mean less than what it seemed?
Were we destined for a cruel fate?

I sometimes believe meeting you was my karmic debt because I had finally met another part of my soul, only for it to abandon me again.

Velvet Eclipse

The idea of moving on and forgetting you is excruciatingly difficult because to close a chapter is to accept erasure of my soul's carefree nature when we were together. You were the last person to witness that side of me. Nothing from that point forward has been the same. And I've tried everything to numb the pain. Believe me, I've tried to forget your name. They tell me to move on, a sense of futility lingering below the surface whispering that nobody will ever understand me like you do. And they don't. I know they won't. My most vibrant memories are tied to who we used to be within the hues of mutual chemistry. Nothing has been the same since. And I know each second of reminiscence isn't allowing my heart space to pick up the pieces, but this spiral of nostalgia brings me an immense amount of peace. Maybe this is what it feels like to be unhealed. Maybe this is what it's like to wake up and never want to fall back asleep.

Samira Vivette

We shared the same darkness.

Call it madness.

I call it magic.

Velvet Eclipse

I could probably
let go if I wanted to.
I could bury the
thought of you,
the idea of us.
Or at least that's
what I tell myself.
My desires hide
behind the illusion
of choice.

It was never about
self-control.

The heart wants
what it wants –
and it will make
it known.

Samira Vivette

Maybe,
if I miss you enough,
you'll feel a heaviness,
an ache whispering
my name all the way
over there and
miss me back.

Velvet Eclipse

Here I am, making space for this longing and its refusal to leave. Here I remain, seeking stillness within the hues of reality between what is and what could have been.

I've drowned in it. I've been consumed by it. Now I sit with the fragments that continue to follow me with acceptance and embracement of their immortality.

Samira Vivette

Why do I have this feeling
we were meant for more,
and our story is far from over?

Nocturnal Stillness

My late-night thoughts of you are quiet, caressing, fragmentary, and merciless. At a certain hour when the sirens are drowned by the whispers of nightfall, it feels like the world is coming to an end because you're no longer in it. I feel nothing and everything all at once. Both auras twirling freely, weightless and uninterrupted, our fingertips find companionship in each other's grip while we reconcile in a realm invisible to the naked eye.

Samira Vivette

It was you when I met you. It was you after we parted. And it is you, even after all this time, in between these memories. It's always going to be you. The moments I truly have to myself are short-lived because my mind, the signs which surround me will not let my mind drift. What does it take? For someone to claw themselves so deep into your psyche that you're left with nothing but their energy and the searing pain of the absence of it. I don't ask myself this question anymore. All I know is I can't let go. And the more I try, the more I'm met with resistance from the outside world. Something is telling me to hold on. I don't know how long for. I'm unsure how much longer I can keep doing this alone.

Velvet Eclipse

With every person I meet,
I become more and more sure of one truth:
There will never be another soul
who understands me like you do.

It's just a phase.
I still haven't met anyone
who can take your place.
It's just a phase.
I gave up on finding
a similar connection
after we parted ways.

Something in me died that day.

You remain blissfully unaware
of the agony I experienced.
I turned inward after our final goodbye,
wrapping my vulnerability in barbed wire.

I didn't want anyone if it wasn't you.
I don't want anyone if it isn't you.

I'd prefer to take
this chance on myself
and cherish the
jagged pieces of glass
guarding my heart
than to let another
into this world
we created for us.

Velvet Eclipse

I lost a part of myself in you.

And by that I don't mean
I now am or was ever incomplete.

After you, my heart forfeited the strength
to seek what we shared in someone else.

I don't know if I'll ever gather the ability
to fall the same way again.

Samira Vivette

I wonder why your memory still has this much of a hold over me. I wish I could be given a reason as to why the significance of your presence in my life still leaves me unable to breathe most nights.

Why won't you leave? Why does the thought of you not being here incapacitate me? I was doing fine before I met you. I had known love. I had experienced loss. And within the breaks of the breeze, I found the strength to move on. But this. This is different. It's almost like you've become a permanent part of me, and I cannot run from this feeling. What have you done to me?

Velvet Eclipse

In every dimension,
in every universe,
in every lifetime,
I promise,
I'll come find you.

And although
we couldn't make it
work in this one,
it doesn't mean
every second
of my existence
won't be spent
wondering why fate
dealt me a hand
so cruel.

Samira Vivette

It's not like I sit around
and think about you
all day long.
You're more a thought
I can't get rid of.
There'll be moments
when I'm having the time of my life
around people I love,
and that emotion invokes one
I felt when I was by your side.
There will be days when our song
plays on shuffle on my playlist
of over a thousand songs,
and in that instance,
you're all I'm thinking of
during the car ride home.
You're always there in some way,
in either the background or foreground.

Velvet Eclipse

I silently await the day
your memory doesn't haunt
my thoughts in any form at all.

But this longing, it is immortal.
I don't think you'll ever leave my mind.

Not in this lifetime.

Samira Vivette

Leave our memories in my hands.
They will never fade into nothingness
as long as I am around.

Velvet Eclipse

Nothing has been
the same since I lost you.
I guess the odds were
always against us,
but I really didn't want
to believe it.

I think, to this day,
I fixate on our potential
more than anything.
I'm left filling in the blanks
of all the memories we had
yet to make –
all the experiences
we never shared.

I wish it turned out different.
I can't stop imagining the impossible.

Synchronicities

It is growing impossible to function in day-to-day life while trying to ignore the signs I'm still on your mind. I see you everywhere, even when I'm not thinking of you, even when I'm focused on something else. You won't leave me alone.

Something is compelling me not to forget you.

Velvet Eclipse

I don't know if I'm missing what we were
or what I hoped we could've been.

All I know is nothing is the same without you here.

Samira Vivette

Tonight, melancholy is overpowering me as I release resistance of a nostalgia I've tried with all my might to suppress. All I want to do is tell you how much I still love you, how much I never stopped. You'll always be my person. You'll always be the one my heart yearns for. Nothing has changed. And believe me, I also hate that it hasn't. Every single day.

Velvet Eclipse

I think it would be
an easier pill to swallow
if our differences were
the reason it all fell apart.

But it's a different kind of pain
to know our similarities
led to our demise.

Samira Vivette

Moving on?

It's not that simple.
Oh, but I wish it were.

I wish I could acknowledge our separation through the lens of luminescence and not a seething longing for what once was. I wish I retained faith in the process and my conflicting emotions hadn't blurred. At the mercy of your touch, they were anything but. Stone-cold waves of electricity melting between our fingers. Intellectual lightning. Tongues tying us both to a land of ecstasy, tenderness laced with magic.

We were magic.

I remember telling myself when it was over between us that I would wait for you to come back, however long it took. And at the time, that sentiment just felt so right. Then after I sat on it for a while, it started to feel pathetic. Not because my feelings had changed, but because I was holding hope for someone who would've still been with me if they wanted to be.

What a barbaric conflict you put me through. I tossed and turned at the idea of even meeting someone new so as not to taint the ghost trails of our lips under the full moon. I preserved our memory as best I could and that involved many sleepless nights closing my eyes and praying my dreams would send me back to you.

It pains me to say my first instinct was the true calling of my heart, and it was my mind that later intervened. Because after all this time, you're still the only one I want.

You've always been the only one for me.

Samira Vivette

There isn't a day
that goes by
where you're
not on my mind.

For you,
my longing
is ongoing.

*We are frozen
in time.*

Velvet Eclipse

Some of us are lucky
enough to experience the
once in a lifetime connection.

And some of us are
equally unlucky in losing it
as we learn to live with
the emptiness.

Samira Vivette

They came to terms with the silence in a way familiar to them. They probably sought companionship from a bottle of gin, a temporary body, an impermanent belief they could move on. Maybe for a moment, they did. But when a connection is spiritually fated, the realization eventually hits. And it doesn't play nice. It waits for a pause, a collapse of thoughts, pouncing on the edge of invincibility and insecurity – when pleasure outmanoeuvres the senses temporarily until the next time solitude hits. Distraction is the side piece that establishes inferiority beside reality. And when the latter hits, regret comes to take what's rightfully owed.

Velvet Eclipse

Sometimes it does take distance. It takes time apart to realize just how special that person was. It takes time apart to validate what you felt was real when the emotions linger over the years. It takes time apart to know with certainty there isn't another like them. And it's a conflicting predicament I'm in because I never needed to be apart from you to know this. Maybe you did. Maybe you didn't. I guess some questions remain unanswered. This is something I'm still trying to figure out how to live with.

I'm over you.
I ran into someone
who looks like you.
I'm over you.
Our song plays
on shuffle
out of the blue.
I'm over you.
The flashbacks
still haunt me.
I'm over you.
There's a flavor
to your memory.
I'm over you.
These goosebumps
betray me.
I'm over you.
I'm over you.
I'm over you.
The ending word
of that sentence
is the only one
I pay attention to.
The rest is static
I convince myself
exists to make
me feel better
about losing you.

Wasteland

I held on with everything that I am.

I've been holding onto us with a brittle heart and eyes swollen with tears until the view of the past flashed past my window. The burst of vibrancy that was once you and me has turned hazy, and I cannot make out anything other than the silhouette of neglected memories. We don't know each other anymore. The space where our worlds once collided with late-night thoughts, intimacy, and tangled dreams is now a wasteland of what could have been.

Samira Vivette

There's not a corner in my mind you don't occupy. I've accepted my real enemy as time because every day that passes us by is another opportunity for the world to keep us apart permanently. You see, I don't know if this radio silence between us has led to you forgetting me completely or missing me in the same capacity. Isn't it unbelievably tragic how delicate a connection can be when seemingly unbreakable memories can fade with the wind?

Velvet Eclipse

I hope you know
you were the last.
You witnessed
the peaks of the
intensity of my
vulnerability.
I let you into
a space of my soul
I never allowed
anyone else.
Do with that
what you will,
but you were
the only one to get
earth-shatteringly close.
Nothing will be
the same again.
I can't do it to myself.

Samira Vivette

Sometimes,
it hurts to breathe
at the thought of your memory
because you're not here.

You're not here with me.

And so, here I am,
stitched together with
false hope and melancholy,
with the ache of grief
that now knows me longer
than you ever did.

Velvet Eclipse

Midnight wraps me in a blanket of isolation with rope tied around my wrists, engulfed in dreams that make me yearn for a life unlived. I can still feel your touch after a certain hour when silence transforms into my foremost companion. With echoes resounding tones of loneliness and goosebump-inducing memories, I am reminded of the delight that consumed me when you were here. I won't allow remembrance to take a back seat because its existence is the only reason I can continue to feel you among these sheets.

Samira Vivette

I just don't see you
having our connection
with anyone else.

And this is not coming
from a place of delusion
or denial because if we really
weren't special, I promise
I'd swallow that pill.

But I just know what I know.
I'm speaking on what I've lived.
You can't feel what we did
and act like it meant nothing.
There is nobody I've ever let
into my soul quite as much as you,
and none of them have or could make
me feel a fraction of the way you do.

Velvet Eclipse

I can only describe
our separation as
catastrophic.

Our connection
comes around
once in a lifetime
and we lost it.

Still, there's a
minuscule flame
within that believes
it's not the end
just yet.

Samira Vivette

They say the past is dead and gone, but the glacial whisper of the breeze tells me if our souls were to reconcile, I'd melt into the cosmos of your body heat like a day had not passed. I could lie to myself and reinforce the ideal that we are a relic of melancholy – a lesson I needed to learn on this journey, an imprint of yesterday's mistakes, but that would mean these feelings would slip through the net of the present and disappear into nothingness. It would mean we no longer exist. But you see, I cannot facilitate erasure of something that has changed the way I see, the way I feel, the depth in which I fall at heights I cannot control. This connection has altered me permanently with a touch most vibrant. And I cannot allow the past to have that.

I need this to remain tangible.

Velvet Eclipse

It's not that I'm waiting
around for you in some
hopeless fashion.

It's more so
nobody after you
has been able
to steal the air
from my lungs.
No voice yet,
no conversation
has been capable
of matching ours.

Nothing now really
catches my attention.

Everything after you
just feels surface-level.

Samira Vivette

You were the only one
who ever felt like home.

And I'll probably spend
eternity trying to recreate
what we had, and it will
forever fall short.

Velvet Eclipse

And I'll aim
to forget you
in another
lifetime.

Samira Vivette

I pledge my loyalty to this feeling of grief you've gifted me because without it, the last thing connecting me to you is gone. There are some mornings I wake up and my eyesight is clearer, my breaths are deeper, and for a split second, just a split second, I really do feel this is my fresh start. I feel one step closer to freedom, to a life where my chest does not ache at the thought of your name, but I am pulled back into this melancholic array of circumstances I wish I could change. I do like it here.

It's strangely comforting. As soon as I step outside of this box, I feel lighter but ever so slightly emptier. I guess I've chosen contentment accompanied by misery only because of familiarity. I know it's not the best place to be. But it's the only source of comfort that replicates the very thing that is no longer here.

Velvet Eclipse

Nobody has ever
touched my soul
the way you have.

And it's impossible for me
to seek someone new because
you awakened a part of my heart
that only now beats for you.

Samira Vivette

It may come across as hopelessly unrequited to keep writing about us like this. I should've moved on by now. I should've tucked my heart back into my sleeve. And I feel that way, sometimes.

But it's the in between.

It's the goosebumps that form to remind me of those late-night conversations we had all the way up until three. It's the way I melted underneath you with nerves firing beneath my skin. It's all the times we finished each other's sentences and agreed upon certain sentiments. It's the afternoons we spent in each other's arms until we both fell asleep. My recollections are candlelit in nature, dimly diffused in the distance – and I'm not fixating on you every second of every day. But there are moments that peek through the crevices that hold my face with the same tenderness and roughness you once did, leading me back down the rabbit hole of hauntingly beautiful recollections and melancholy.

And so, this longing has become an inevitable part of my existence because you touched a part of my soul that had been buried in cobwebs for as long as I've been alive. And I just can't let go of that. I can't let go of us.

Velvet Eclipse

I wish
I knew
if I was on
your mind.

And I wonder
if you wonder
about just how
much you're
still on mine.

Samira Vivette

I write because I'm over what you did to me and the way you left and how I thought you were the one before you tore me to shreds. I write because you're not my last thought before I go to bed and how every ounce of your essence doesn't flow through my veins. I write to remember you because you're someone I could easily forget. I write because when it comes to you, I'm a master of lying to myself.

Velvet Eclipse

If I can feel
your energy,
why won't
you reach
out to me?

But then again,
I'm here trying to
forget your name,
asking myself why
I can't do the
same thing.

Samira Vivette

When the space between nights spent collapsing into my pillow became shorter, I knew it wasn't an overreaction. When enough time had passed for any logical person to move on and the Universe wasn't letting me, I surrendered. When the intensity of this connection failed to falter after coping in the only ways I knew how, I decided to let it take me. I made the conscious choice to ride this wave, no matter how long it would take. I am in no position to forget this lesson, to move on from you just yet. My mind, my body, my spirit won't let it happen, and who am I to go against them?

Velvet Eclipse

I don't regret
falling into you,
falling into us.

But maybe
I do regret,
just a little bit,
holding onto hope
our last time together
wouldn't have been
the last.

Samira Vivette

One day you'll understand why I couldn't bring myself to return your message. Please leave me be. Melancholy has replaced everything we could ever be, and I am happy in this misery. It's a feeling I couldn't even explain to you if I tried, but the idea of you in my head is untouched, free from the twisted sting of reality. Trust me, it's better this way. Remember me how I once was. You don't want to reignite what we had. I'm afraid the part of me you seek is in a state of decay. But it's beautiful in every way. A kind of beauty you could never appreciate.

I know this is real because ever since I met you, I haven't been able to stop thinking about you, even after all this time – even in the silence.

Especially in the silence.

Samira Vivette

And if only
you were here
to come home to
after I finally
came home
to myself.

I never held onto hope that time would heal me, but my mind had been open to the possibility. And now that so much has passed, I'm left thinking how one person can have such an impact on one's psyche. It's not that my entire night involves sitting on my bedroom floor for hours grieving what we were. I mean, not anymore. It's not that I'm consciously wanting this to ensue. Life goes on. And life has reminded me of that several times, even if I never thought it would. Ever since we parted ways, you've become a thought that never truly leaves. You're the witty stranger I meet on the street. You're the romantic movie scene. You're the warmth in my chest. You're everything I miss but can't have. Maybe in an alternate reality, we are by each other's sides. Maybe in an alternate universe, time never had a chance to prove itself right.

Samira Vivette

I don't know if you miss me
as much as I miss you,
but I hope wherever you are,
whatever you're doing,
that your heart is full.

Velvet Eclipse

One day, I just may stop thinking of you and replaying the possibilities of everything we could still be.

But until that day comes, if it ever does, I have our memories and melancholy keeping me company.

Samira Vivette

I believe that
if we're meant to be,
our paths will lead us
to the same place
again someday.

We found each
other once already,
and I know we can do it again.

And so, the stars shall mind our fate,
illuminating all the possibilities
of the memories still to be shared.

Velvet Eclipse

There is an immortality woven between the threads of our memories. My heart yearns for us at the height of our happiness, but my soul knows we will forever be attached energetically.

Samira Vivette

It's as simple as the fact we both just weren't ready. I'm always justifying in my mind the concept of the right person, wrong time, but if it was meant to be, wouldn't things be vastly different? Wouldn't the middle have sounded like a nice place to meet? There could have been more working in our favor, but it seemed the odds were against us right from the beginning. Our lives ended up following two different trajectories. But when we met, we were on the same one which led to our collision. And I'm coming to terms with this. I'm trying to accept the fact that we were too similar in many ways, and this space very well could have led to us growing apart into unrecognizable people to each other.

I'll always miss who we were.

Velvet Eclipse

I really do wish you nothing but the best. Your presence triggered a myriad of unhealed wounds within myself, and it was only after the eye of the storm passed that I was able to make peace with the debris.

I wish we could have met now.

But I also know it isn't meant to work like that.

I can only hope our second chance leads us toward a path we are ready to walk together.

Samira Vivette

You will likely meet someone new. And the same thing that happened to me will happen to you. The months will pass to our mutual relief or dismay while distraction takes the reins. And you'll lose yourself in what you feel is a fresh start. Until the novelty dissipates. Until the feeling that something is missing cannot be shaken. And such a realization won't be evident on the surface. In fact, life may even feel lighter, a touch more joyous. But there will be an inescapable desolation, a space that cannot be reached by anybody else – a semicolon hovering above your shoulders in shades of neon. Time will reveal what we always knew but never cared to admit with passion.
I know this because we keep finding our way back to each other. The scales always tip in our favor.

Velvet Eclipse

I ask myself if we were to still know each other after this time apart.

But then I remember all the moments I found an old souvenir in my drawers and how the memories flooded my bones like I had first set my eyes upon it.

I know that in this life, change is the only constant. But I also know when something is special, and both souls share a unique kind of magic, the bond remains infinite.

Samira Vivette

I've made peace with the fact it is always going to be you. It was the moment I met you. It still is all this time after. And I don't want to even think about what's to come because as it stands, I cannot let anybody else in to the same extent. I physically can't.

Velvet Eclipse

Maybe one day we'll recognize each other again in the same light when our worlds first collided. Maybe enough time will pass where our mistakes are entwined underneath our skin as we promise rebellion of the same ones that led to our separation. Maybe one day your gaze will tell me the same things it did those nights we were unstoppable. Maybe hostility undergoes a transformation toward non-existence. Maybe familiarity and longing fill the space between us as voices of reason reinforcing what we chose to give up as the ultimate lesson to never be so careless again.

Samira Vivette

Enough time
has passed for
me to move on
with my life,
to leave the idea
of us behind –
but no matter
how hard I try,
you just won't
leave my
mind.

Velvet Eclipse

I know it's not infatuation.
I know it's not a phase.
How can it be when
I've met others
before *and* after you,
and still to this day,
nobody can take
your place?

Samira Vivette

One day,
you will meet
someone with
wounds as deep
as yours –
a wandering soul
left in the cold
by everyone
they've ever
known.

And together,
you'll create
a home with
the warmth
neither of you
were ever
shown.

Velvet Eclipse

I miss the person I was when we were together – a spirit so endearingly thoughtless, entwined with the right amount of naivety, wanting to see the best in everything… unquestioning, welcoming, recklessly wild on the edge of remembering and forgetting, chasing thrills in spades without regard of consequence or guarantee of tomorrow. Soulfully alive. There she was, cherishing retention of a certain flicker of immortality, scarring every corner of her heart. We remain etched in memory in those very moments because after you, I was nobody else's again. A seemingly melodramatic statement proved validity in the space of isolation while refusing formation of a connection other than the one we shared.

Samira Vivette

I think you'd be happy for me. I finally found myself at the expense of losing everything that I thought I wouldn't survive without. Truth be told, I almost didn't make it out alive. The loss I've experienced was almost enough to obliterate me. But when you and I parted ways, a portion of my resilience endured a rot that still lingers to this day. There is nothing aesthetic or palatable about the purge that followed your departure. I kept asking myself why I had to meet you when I did, when an aura of healing felt like it was waiting for me to turn a corner. My bloodstream consisted of rage and resentment for not being gifted more time with you, more nights where everything around us came to a standstill. I miss the intimate intoxication. I miss the late-night conversation. I miss the cheap, priceless moments together where nothing really mattered. I miss not having to miss it.

Velvet Eclipse

Why won't the Universe let me forget you?
I've tried. I'm trying.
But it doesn't matter what I do.

Something keeps calling me back to you.

Samira Vivette

I hope that one day you find the love I found in you. I hope your mornings are weightless and your nights are limitless, and I hope the sky adopts a brighter shade of blue. I hope you see the beauty in unpredictability and nourish the fragments of intensity within the depths of your being. I hope your heart feels the same way toward this world as mine does for you. I wish for color to accompany your grays and sunshine to transform all of your regrets into recollections of a life well-lived. I can only hope the soul mine has adored since the moment we crossed paths finds its happiness. Even if that happiness isn't me.

Velvet Eclipse

Is there any possibility, in any sort of logic-defying reality, you hear my heart apologizing to yours?

Samira Vivette

It will never
not be you.

And I'm still trying
to make peace with this
because my heart
refuses to.

Velvet Eclipse

I know why we needed to separate.
I now know there were some lessons
we needed to learn apart.
But nothing can dull the ache
which took your place.

I miss you more
than words can convey.

Samira Vivette

We found each other once,
and we'll find each other again
if fate decides we're meant to be.

I have this idea in my head of our future reunion. I picture an air of understanding, two spirits reconciling, and divulging the time spent apart while our thoughts still drifted in each other's direction. I perceive an emotional weightlessness and acknowledgement – the certainty that fate had held us apart until certain lessons were learned. In the same breath, I ponder if this will ever happen, and when I do reach the stage of acceptance, if I would have moved on by then. The heart can only take so much. At least that's what I tell myself. But it's this very thought that keeps me going even if it will never happen. I need to believe I'll see you somehow again. Even if it's the furthest from the truth. You came back. In some alternate reality, you come back. And the fragments left here have since disappeared. It's almost as if you hadn't left at all. My tea is still sweetened with the same amount of sugar. My eyelids are still puffy in the morning. I still leave everything behind some afternoons and chase isolated roads with the windows down and my hair blowing across my eyes. You still know me. This version never left.

Samira Vivette

I will not hopelessly
wait around for you.
I will continue to live my life
and ensure it is as fulfilling
and wonderful as possible.
Nostalgia will keep me company,
as will the warmth of our memories.
And here I am, making new ones.

But the way I feel about you
will never change.
It's the one thing I'm certain of.

It's true.
My life will go on without you.
And it will be spectacular and
awe-inspiring and beautiful.
But it doesn't mean there won't always be
an indescribable emptiness within,
that speck of a void only you can fill.

It doesn't mean I won't search for you
in everyone I meet who's *just not you.*

The Reunion…

Velvet Eclipse

You will find me one day, I'm sure.

When my phone number isn't in service anymore and the mailbox you once recognized belongs to a family of four. When the sting of our final conversation adopts a feeling that is bittersweet instead of haunting.

If the stars happen to align for us down the line, you'll know where to find me. You can follow the whisper within the confines of your soul, the one familiar with my voice, and you can make your way back home into my arms.

I will be waiting for you, darling.

Samira Vivette

I fell in love with your flaws.

And I think the realization that consoled my spirit wasn't that you weren't perfect.

It's that you're the same shade of imperfect as I am.

Velvet Eclipse

I let you back in
because nobody else
could ever come close.

I let you back in
because nothing
was the same since
we parted.

I let you back in
because I no longer
could deny the truth
to myself.

I let you in again,
not because I need you,
but because I adore you.

Samira Vivette

It's different
with you.
It always was.

And I knew,
well before
we drifted apart,
nothing could ever
match what we had.
Nobody else
yields the power
to break these
walls down.
No other soul
can untangle
this heart.

It's different now,
perpetually.

Reserved for you,
and you only,
is a mutual existence
of longing and agony.

Velvet Eclipse

I don't always believe what I see. I believe what I feel. I believe in a spiritual complexity that far overrides what is visible in this current dimension. Life has taught me repeatedly that nothing is ever black or white. And I'm constantly residing within the hues of gray. You can be in love with someone and walk away. Silence can be the path taken alluding to an absence of feelings when the voiceless is left crumbling. Reunions occur in due time if fate is ever so inclined. Sometimes souls are forced into separation to learn lessons that could not be learned together. Sometimes we say what we don't mean. Sometimes we don't say what we really think. We humans are not cut from a perfect cloth. The signs around us will both guide and reassure us of our seemingly impossible thoughts. Our emotions are validated if one pays close enough attention. We are all imperfect – inherently contradictory, chaotic spirits finding the best path to navigate. And each of us hone a mess within that is uniquely ours to cherish.

Samira Vivette

The months are passing.
The years are flying.
Everything is changing.
Loving you has been
the only constant.

Velvet Eclipse

There is a feeling within that screams with certainty that I'll always find my way back to you.

In the space between moments, when I am at my highest or my lowest, it's you.

It has always been *you*.

Samira Vivette

The cycle of our past reunion came around like clockwork. We had found each other yet again during the peak of our individual breakthroughs. I was undergoing a period of immense growth, as were you.

Since our separation, nothing has been the same in the most wonderful of ways. I see the world with a new lens. I no longer resonate with the version of me that you knew.

This healed version of me is pretty damn cool.
I wish you were here to meet her too.

And I just wanted to say the one thing that hasn't changed is I'm still thinking of you. I just can't stop. I often reflect on how great it would be to share stories and bond over how naive we were, how far we've both come. But I know it isn't the right time to reconcile just yet, if at all.

But I sincerely hope life is great for you.
My heart really misses yours.

Velvet Eclipse

I was in love once. And you probably wouldn't believe me if I told you a connection of the same caliber never came around again. I never opened my heart after that. My walls refused to lower. But it didn't matter. I never could settle for someone, anyone after them. My appreciation remained among the wreckage thereafter. I sought nothing and embraced everything. My faith in divine intervention remained unwavering. This heart took solace in solitude and wept to every solemn tune. Every shooting star spelled their name. I let fate take the reins. I couldn't bring myself to be with just anyone. Because nobody was them. I was in an existence-questioning, bone-shattering, cataclysmic love once. And its remnants alone are enough for me to live the rest of my life untouched.

Samira Vivette

I really believe the Universe
ensures we never forget certain people.

I believe in connection
even when it's not always visible.

Velvet Eclipse

I promise I will find you when the time is right. I need to ensure these loose ends are tied and this body is no longer in a state of repair. I need to make sure you are not collateral damage. I need to grow into the best version of myself.

I promise I'll come back for you. I promise the color of every sunrise and the glow of every star will continue to resemble your essence in your absence. I promise you will see me in every constellation, hear my voice in the afternoon breeze, feel my warmth comforting your energy when you feel lonely.

I never left. But I need to sort out what's in my head.
I need to ensure what happened the last time we were together doesn't happen again.

Samira Vivette

Darling, there will always be a part of his heart reserved for me. I claim this with certainty. I do not say this lightly. Distance doesn't mean shit when there is an underlying connection so intense, so potent it claws its way beneath one's psyche. Our mutual intensity brings us back to each other every damn time. Absence is not the decider. The wildness of our spirits ensure we both wander. But we always find our way back to each other. You cannot permanently intervene between a twin flame connection.

That morning.

As we welcomed the sunrise after the thunderstorm that was our collision, earthy tones and hazel hues blending until our longing ran dry, I could finally say after all this time, right then and there, you were mine.

If only for a few moments.

I know I wasn't the only one in that space.
You knew you weren't the only one in that space.

My cheeky proclamation of comparison
was met with a breathless declaration…
I don't kiss anyone the way I kiss you.

And I swear, you've never kissed me like that before.
And I couldn't help but lean into you with everything that I am,
and I couldn't slow down if I tried.

I just cannot slow down.
Not with you.

And everything afterward doesn't need to make sense.

Because I felt the way you felt after all this time.

And I know my body explained it better than I ever could.

Samira Vivette

That night.
I will never forget that night.

I will never forget how you held me,
how we danced in your living room until three,
our minds a euphoric daze—a paid visit from nostalgia
closing the gap between blistering longing and reunion.

If only you knew
how much I missed you,
how much I couldn't stop
thinking about you.

Glass reflections capturing mist, our limbs in heavenly bliss,
she left your lips, pirouetting past mine, ever so soothingly.

There we were, confined within four walls,
experiencing weightlessness as one,
locking eyes within a swirl leading us beyond infinity.

The crushed weight of past mistakes and disarray
evaporated with the same urgency as our memory of
what it felt like to be apart.

Right then and there,
we were completely
and wholeheartedly…

untouched.

Velvet Eclipse

I'm in the early stages of acceptance.
And this doesn't mean my heart aches any less,
but I have surrendered any sense of control
I thought I had in the matter.

The Universe knows what is best for me.

Whatever is meant to be will be...
and I'm blessed to experience this journey.

Samira Vivette

It was always you –
from the moment
I met you.

And every moment
thereafter.

Velvet Eclipse

Some souls
we can't forget
no matter how
hard we try.

And there is always
a reason for it,
even if not in sight.

The Universe will fight
for the stars to align,
despite how much time
passes us by.

Samira Vivette

The one
who is meant for you
might wander,
get lost,
lose track of time
for a while,
find solace in
distraction
while you
grieve
alone.
But they
will *always*
find their way
back home.

They will always
find their way
back home.

Velvet Eclipse

I loved you despite it all.

And that's something you can never take from me.

Samira Vivette

The memories
are always a little more
vibrant after midnight.

Velvet Eclipse

Here we are, together again, in one another's essence like it never happened. Here we are yet again like our separation was a speck of our imagination, and my nights without you weren't spent with mascara-stained cheeks, repetitive tunes of melancholy, and diary entries. Here I am, telling you everything you missed while you were away from me. Here we are, sharing stories, wisdom, synchronicities, falling into laughter, whispering under the full moon, exposing secrets and mistakes which could have been made a lifetime ago. Here we lie, reunited among a continual glow, knowing what is meant for us will always return.

Thank you for reading.

I hope my words resonated with you in some form, and you found healing and comfort within these pages.

If you enjoyed reading my book, it would be appreciated if you can leave a review on Amazon.

Love,

Samira

www.ingramcontent.com/pod-product-compliance
Lightning Source LLC
Chambersburg PA
CBHW022018290426
44109CB00015B/1213